The Universe Project

poems by

**Diane Allerdyce, Andrea Best,
Gene Martel, and Jeff Morgan**

Finishing Line Press
Georgetown, Kentucky

The Universe Project

Credits: NASA, ESA and J. Olmsted (STScI)

Copyright © 2025 by Diane Allerdyce, Andrea Best, Gene Martel, and Jeff Morgan
ISBN 979-8-89990-260-4 First Edition
All rights reserved under International and Pan-American Copyright Conventions. No part of this book may be reproduced in any manner whatsoever without written permission from the publisher, except in the case of brief quotations embodied in critical articles and reviews.

ACKNOWLEDGMENTS

Earlier versions of Diane Allerdyce's "Universe and Dormitas" and "Missing," and the current versions of "The Perpetual Flood" and "There is Still Love: A Poem for Haiti, January 12, 2010" appear previously in her book of poetry and prose, *House of Aching Beauty (EditionsPerleDesAntilles*, 2012). Andrea Best's "The Transit of Venus" appears in Quest: Lynn University Literary and Arts Journal (2004). Gene Martel's "Fog" appears in an early version in *Candelabrum* (2002). Jeff Morgan's "Magdalenian" appears previously in *Pinyon* (2016) and "Jupiter Shone" in *The Midnight Oil* (2018).

All images are from websites for the European Space Agency and NASA, including imagery from Apollo, the International Space Station, Hubble, the Space Telescope Science Institute, the Jet Propulsion Laboratory, the Solar Dynamics Observatory, and the Goddard Space Flight Center with additional online imagery from the Event Horizon Telescope Network, the Carnegie Institute for Science, and National Park Service. Additional information is captioned.

Publisher: Leah Huete de Maines
Editor: Christen Kincaid
Cover Art: NASA, ESA, S Beckwith (STScI), and the HUDF Team
Author Photos: Andrea Best (Andrea Best), Diane Allerdyce (TASCA Studios), Gene Martel (Donna Girouard), and Jeff Morgan (Minerva Carabello)
Cover Design: Elizabeth Maines McCleavy

Order online: www.finishinglinepress.com
also available on amazon.com

Author inquiries and mail orders:
Finishing Line Press
PO Box 1626
Georgetown, Kentucky 40324
USA

Contents

Creation 1
    Star Stuff 2
    They Say That There's a Schemer 4
    First Cause 6
    Galactic Longing 8
    Singularity 10
    Wonder 11
    The Big Rip 12
    A Victimless Crime 13
    This Meeting 14
    Eternal Oneness 16
    Universe and Dormitas 17

The Sun 23
    Magdalenian 24
    Angry Sun 25
    The Sun and the Moon 27
    Waking to Other Voices 29
    Fog 31
    Gliding Through 33

Planets 35
    Naked Goddess 36
    The Transit of Venus 37
    A Dream Magnificat 38
    Rogue Planet 39
    Jupiter Shone 40
    On the Edge 41
    A Universe of Corn 42

Satellites 45
    Quantum Entanglement 46
    Tidal Coupling 48
    Panthalassic Embrace 50
    The Perpetual Flood 51
    Oneness 52
    Missing 53

Epilogue 59
    There is Still Love: A Poem for Haiti, January 12, 2011 60
    The Final Theory 62
    To Search the Distant Star 63
    The Missing Link 64

Authors' Bios 65

PREFACE

The Universe Project originated within a longstanding writers' group that met in Palm Beach County beginning in the early 2000s and continued in various configurations for nearly two decades. We called ourselves The Smoking Loon Poetry Society in those days. The name came from a brand of wine we often drank at our meetings.

Sometimes, we gave ourselves assignments. When we were to meet in roughly two weeks, each member was to bring an original poem based on the assignment.

Because we all had a love for science and loved to write about science poetically, one of our assignments became a project. For over two years, meeting at one another's house every two weeks or so, we came with these poems, specifically focusing on the physical branch of science and the category of astronomy. Thus was born our Universe Project.

Like any good writing group, we provided feedback to one another on what we liked and didn't like about our poems on this matter. Over the years, some poems have been revised and some have been published. They play so well together.

CREATION

Credit: NASA, ESA, CSA, STScI; Joseph DePasquale (STScI),
Anton M. Koekemoer (STScI), Alyssa Pagan (STScI).

Star Stuff
by Andrea Best

Though I cannot see you,
I know you are there.
Icy determined traveler,
an indifferent dense darkness
bending space and time before me
to orbit some seductive star.

I feel you
the way you were.
But we are galaxies apart,
unintentional juggernauts
speeding toward some unknown end,
the distance getting cold.

I am circling,
arms outstretched, thinking
we are the stuff of stars.

Can you remember
the birth of our primeval atom
that began with a bang
ten thousand million years ago?

Credit: ESA/Hubble & NASA, J. Tan (Chalmers University & University of Virginia), R. Fedriani

They Say That There's a Schemer
by Gene Martel

They say that there's a schemer scheming schemes,
whose complicated plan is plain to see.
I say that they are dreamers dreaming dreams.
The complex cosmos can't exist, it seems,
by interaction sans a referee.
There has to be a schemer scheming schemes.
They claim a master planner plans and deems
that worlds react and change accordingly.
I claim that they are dreamers dreaming dreams.
Though nature's ever changing chaos gleams,
the scheme holds afterlife eternally.
They say that there's a schemer scheming schemes.
There's motive to invent a god, it seems.
With nothing constant, death's a reality.
I say they must be dreamers dreaming dreams.
This awful universe in turmoil seems.
Its matter was, and is, may always be.
They say that there's a schemer scheming schemes.
I say that they are dreamers dreaming dreams.

Credits: NASA/JPL-Caltech

First Cause
by Jeff Morgan

Bored, His mouth parts
and out dance gasses
into nothing,
and, fearing the worst,
they dance back.
But, the mouth has closed,
leaving them outside forever.

Lonely, the gases combine,
stars shine,
and gas giants twirl
while somewhere out there,
still in the dark,
an old, ugly man mutilates
a young, beautiful woman.

Guilty, as when the patient coughs
his contagion into the world,
infecting those he loves the most,
He chooses death
and becomes like the star
that has drawn its last breath
though looking alive to us.

All this takes a long time, and we forget.

Oblivious, we are abruptly sucked into oblivion.

Credit: NASA

Galactic Longing
by Andrea Best

2.5 million light years of longing—
time to contemplate the consummation
of this cosmic preoccupation.
Time to wonder and plan,
doubt and scheme,
fall in and out of love.
The agony of distance—
relentless attraction,
the closest thing to fate.

Two massive galaxies falling together
as the rest of the universe speeds away.
Without words,
there is only the waiting.
The space between
a cold consequence
of galactic longing.
Patience, not choice
but exigency.

Might they coalesce around
a common loneliness?
So much depends upon
Andromeda's transverse velocity.
Galaxies compelled towards
eternal embrace
enact the inevitable.
Spiral arms outstretched—
two super massive black holes
disturb space
with their dark hearts.

Credit: NASA, ESA, Z. Levay and R. van der Marel (STScI); T. Hallas; and A. Mellinger

Singularity
by Gene Martel

Central to all galaxies
is concentrated gravity.
An imploding, collapsing star's
particles of matter compressed
to finite density and
zero volume as gravity
magnified. Impossible? Maybe,
but close counts in galaxy games.
Billions of stars held in orbit
swirling around a huge Black Hole—
a mighty Singularity!

You, my darling, are singular,
a singularity playing
galaxy games—with hearts of men.
The more you attract, the stronger
the attraction until your heart's
volume approaches zero
its density infinity

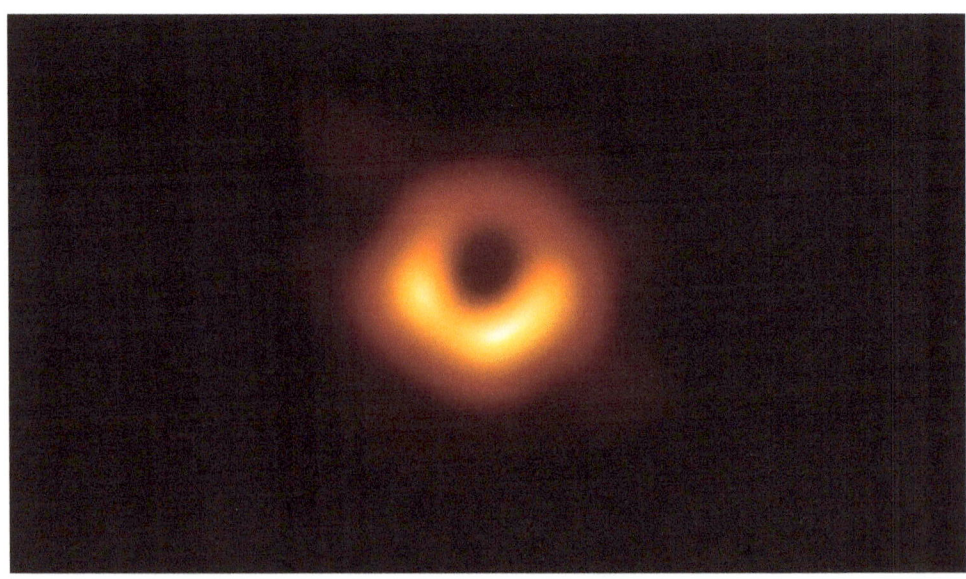

Credit: Event Horizon Telescope

Wonder
by Andrea Best

The idea of him, a novelty—
a distraction, an obsession.
One thought, then another,
and again.
Could it hurt to wonder
what exists out of reach
in some alien world
where he sits
contemplating cosmic confluence?
Maybe he imagines me, too,
sitting here tapping keys
beneath fervid fingertips
dreaming up an alternate universe
where our lives might intersect
in moments, like bubbles—
an adventitious symphony
of vibrating strings

The Big Rip
by Andrea Best

Our bed orbits the center of the universe,
an eidetic image, a prophecy.
Numinous phantom dark energy
infinite acceleration, beautiful—
rips me from your arms.
Libidinous musings,
your favorite shame,
echo in the vast indifference
of space and time
expanding between us.
Maybe it is the years,
your favorite shame
precariously balanced
at the precipice of this dream.
Solar system unbound,
stars and planets cleaved.
The heaviness of our room,
our secrets,
our atoms—
ripped from our arms.

A Victimless Crime
by Andrea Best

They decide
to squeeze the juice
out of each moment,
neglect to check the light switch
and graze a thumb to their teeth.
Instead, blurring the arbitrary line
between reality and a dream,
they traverse the unspoken divide
between two people.

Reaching out beyond oneself, one's life,
to dip a toe in the unknown
depths of some new fascination—
a victimless crime
existing only in the shadows,
confined to the d-brane
of a clandestine universe,
they create upon colliding.

In this quantum embrace
ten dimensions fold upon themselves
only to expand within a
napping neocortex
awakened by neurons firing.
Electrified neurotransmitters
diffuse across a synaptic cleft
exciting a part of them long forgotten.

The law of unintended consequences,
interminable, as the gravity of
what they have begun
warps and perturbs the world
they thought would be unaffected.
First a fullness, then a void.
One brief, ecstatic encounter
now an achromatized recollection
existing only in the mind.

This Meeting
by Andrea Best

> *Each friend represents a world in us, a world possibly not born until they arrive, and it is only by this meeting that a new world is born*
> —Anais Nin

I have been waiting.
I have been waiting.

Placid princess, dormant
as the night blooming cereus.
Her year of polite restraint
forgotten in a moment
as she unfurls—
fragrant, white, and expansive
for only one night.

New friend, unlike the rest
you try yourself on
in my mirror,
let me show you
the world through my eyes.

Time protracted,
deceptively still and reassuring,
seeps through the cracks
along the edges of this dream—
filling the space around me.
I rise to my toes
holding my breath
to dive.

Drenched in the metallic
afterbirth of our creation,
we leave a trail of glistening footprints—
a canvas painted by experience
channeled through convergence zones.
Our memories, fragmented snapshots
tossed in a shoebox
hidden in its right place.

Stories we confess in hushed voices,
words that pollinate the night with
evanescent inventions—
this new language
folds space and time over
where the two of us touch
momentarily.
Mouths silenced by the thrill
of coming together.

Eternal Oneness
by Gene Martel

Eternal oneness shatters momentarily.
Random fragments bond in rich diversity.
Each in a wink of time confronts diversity.
Being holds its shape but temporarily.

Atoms attract and cling momentarily.
Chaos rules transcending regularity.
All in time return to singularity.
Coalesce to oneness solitarily.

Universe and Dormitas
by Diane Allerdyce

I
In the distance the train sounds its low horn,
intricate shards of light crisscrossing sound
and thought across the universe unborn,
the ribbon of track, the ungrounded crown
of earth rising to meet my dream, reeling.
I'm here and aware that I'm here. But why
does this amorphous body feel so distinct
as I sleep? I feel my own skin, the sky
at the edge of my eyelids, pink, calling
the new day forward to the hail and cry
of a songbird. And what is this startling
consciousness of mine? I'll rise now and fly
sky to skyline, cloud to cloud, as you sing
me awake to the morning, my starling.

II
In James Wright's poem the horses cross the field
to greet him. I'm so struck with his image
of how they love each other. They unpeel
their grass surfaces, approach the fence, nudge him
toward a peace beyond and yet intrinsic to
an ordinary knowing. Their soft eyes
contain multitudes, whole worlds vivid, new,
and palpable, sending without disguise
or artifice a message—connection.
Beyond this scene I hear the ocean waves.
I feel them churning, sense their ebb and flow.
They hug the shore as if with affection
like that the poet found in horses' gaze,
each moon a mirror of their eyes below.

III
Under the surface of my parents' pool,
my body its own container, sleek package
relinquishing weight to the safety (cool
respite from heartbreak and the cruel damage
the world has exacted upon us) here
in sudden, unwarned aftermath of loss
beyond our stunned comprehension, I steer
the leaden load, flesh and feeling, across
the Milky Way. And words are flying out
of travailing throats, unwinding cliché.
Surrealistically, they fall. I shout
against maddening truths. They ricochet.
I swim, end to end, galaxies swirling
in a universe of ribbons twirling.

IV
From the tops of all the passengers' heads
in front of me there is something rising,
transparent shimmering translucent threads
of vulnerability and awe surprising
the air above them, with all of the cells of
my body, my heart, kidneys, and liver
responding. Membrane-porous I dissolve,
join all of them in the sentient river,
the gravitational pull of planets,
each living breathing entity in orbit
with and around each other. But can it
keep us from flying out into dormant
unawareness? I think so. Gravity
trends toward kindness as toward sanity.

V
In the pool the children, now grown, throw balls
and laughter as ribbons of memory
wind their rainbow way around the soft walls
of their limbs, skin to water's skin, and see
time elapsing. They don't know I'm thinking this.
We are just here, playing, laughing at love
and youth and the imponderousness
of grown-up children playing push and shove.
I wonder where they've gone, the joys and strife?
They are right here, my loves, my children, rife
with living, full of longing and promise.
It's now decades since I swam my parents'
pool of tears in drowning grief's forbearance.

VI
In the distance the train blows its low horn,
weaving strands of shadow over the sound
of dreams crisscrossed in moonlit fields of corn,
ribbons of waking universe unwound.
There is a drumming in the distant hills
that calls for an answer, for metaphor
and proverb. This burning in my blood kills
any spiritual meandering or
possibility of veering off track.
The mountains rise to meet my dream, reeling.
I'm here and aware. There's no going back
from this place to anywhere less healing.
To you who are out there and listening,
I surrender, newborn and glistening.

VII

As I sleep, I feel my own skin, the sky
at the edge of my eyelids, porous. Pink
as the new day coming, my bones defy
their own too-real fragility and sink
into sleep. The uncounted hours and days
and uncollected nuances blend in,
welding red sea stones to violet fish as waves
descend to join refracted light bent in
the depths at the opening of these caves.
I'm offering everything, severing
all holding. (So, my friends, what should we make
of this strange and passionate hovering
we're pulling off just inches above
where we sit reading poetry we love?)

Credit: NPS/Kait Thomas

THE SUN

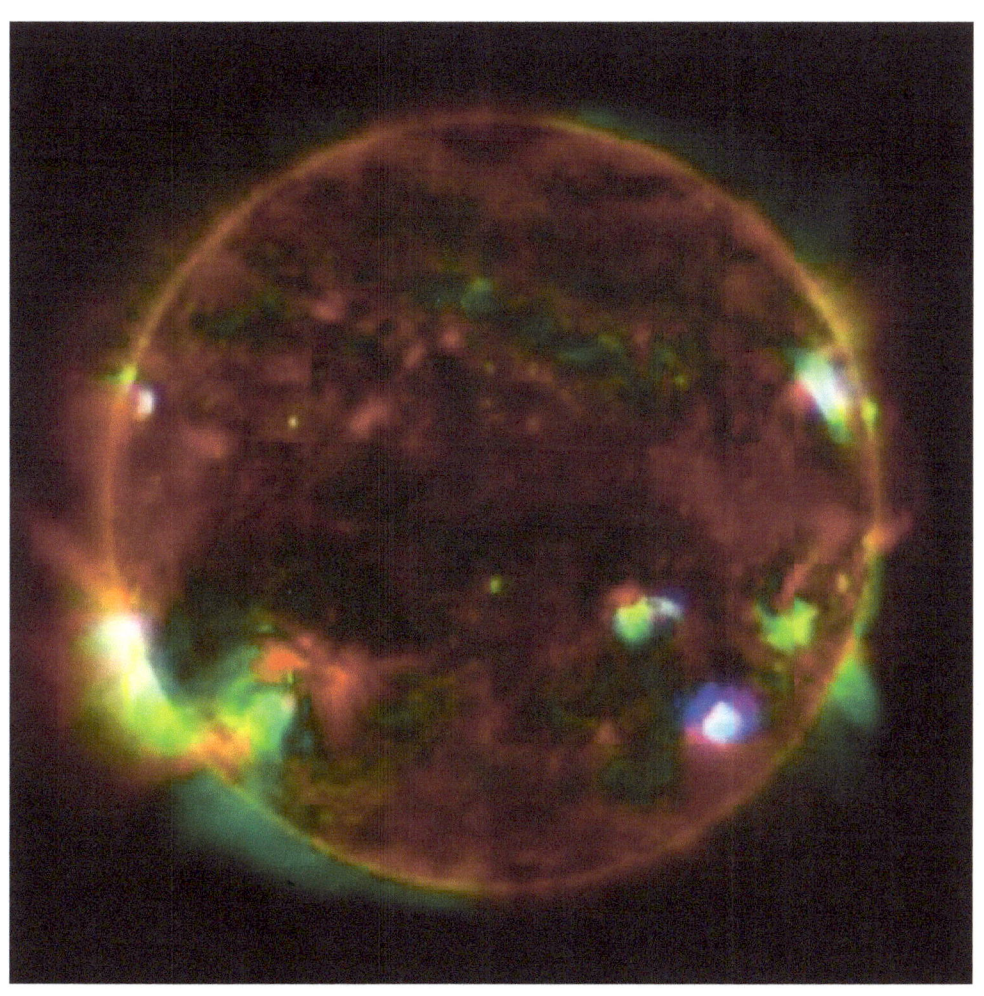

Credit: NASA/JPL-Caltech/JAXA

Magdalenian
by Jeff Morgan

The sun kept rising.
This became as absolute
as her gray father decaying on the rocks.
He is no longer himself.
He does not swat the flies,
and the wind sometimes carries him.
What was once is no more,
but with the sun what is no more is.

She sees a pattern in the moon and the stars,
not a simple fact, but an essay, an analysis
that reveals a cycle, and having witnessed birth,
she makes a womb in the earth
and rolls her father in
while the blood drips down her leg.
So, the absolute became abstract
on the walls of Lascaux.

Angry Sun
by Andrea Best

I thought I would try to understand you
through spectroscopy—
disperse your blinding light through a prism,
see of what you are really made.
Were you the product of some galactic hit and run
left in the wake of some thoughtless supernova?
Or born in a starburst cluster nursing on dark matter?

4.5 billion years ago
inside you, nuclear energy transmuted elements—
Hydrogen and Helium—
releasing photons, your first light.

Time has insulated me
from the brutality of your
coronal mass ejections.
My magnetic force field flexes
in the face of your solar winds,
determined to erode my atmosphere.

Angry sun,
I fear your cacophonous reactions;
yet I bathe in your radiation—
dependent on your indifferent fidelity.

You gave me life,
though I can never get close to you.

You gave me life.
Though inevitably,
you shall take it away.

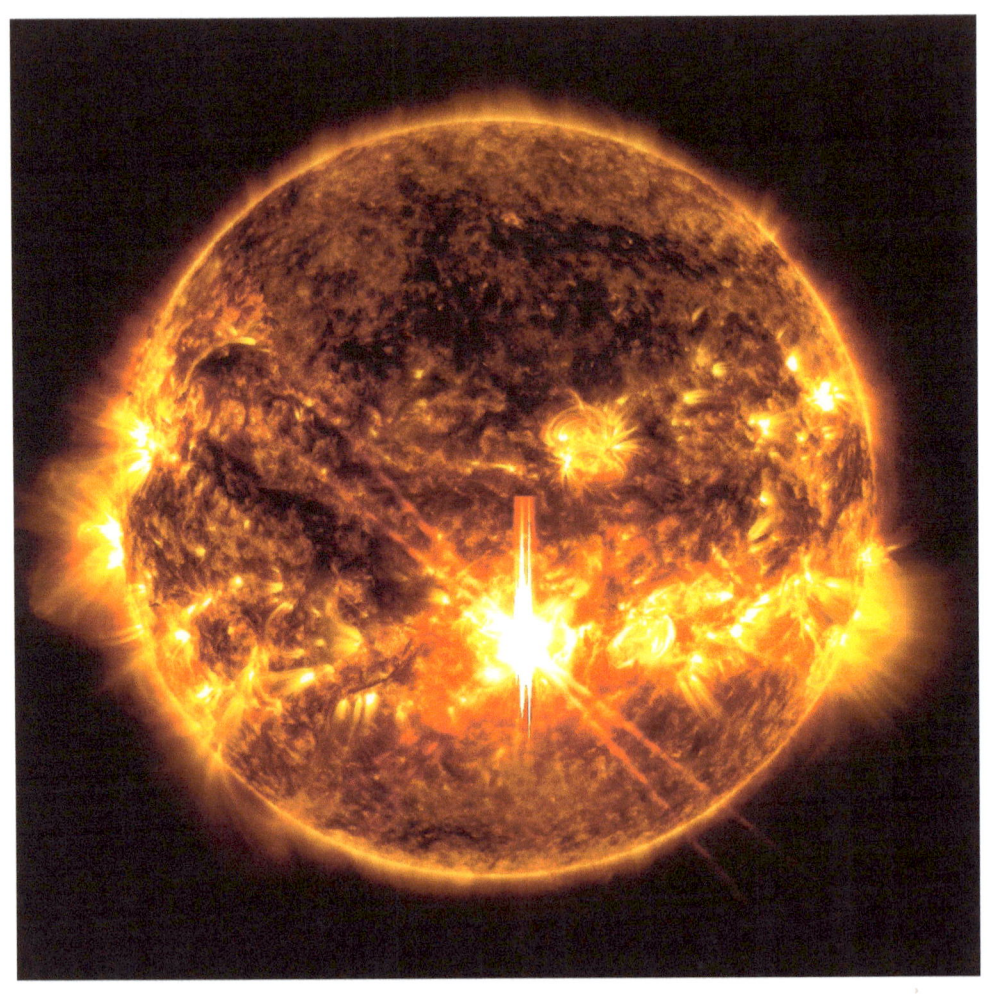

Credit: NASA/SDO

The Sun and the Moon
by Jeff Morgan

The green plants drink the sun,
and the animal eats the green plants,
chewing on the sun
until the bone of one of his own
comes crashing through his skull,
causing flashes of bright lights,
more brilliant than a thousand suns,
to momentarily shine before all becomes black.

That night, the dawn of culture rises around the fire
that mimics the sun,
lighting their small world,
warming their bodies,
feeding their bodes
with the flesh of the sun
as they chant, tell stories,
and draw raw pictures in the dirt with sticks.

But, unseen, in the dark, at the roots of a tree,
a fungus, shunning the sun, rises from the earth to release it spores
under the moon,
and one man partakes of the offering,
causing flashes of bright lights
more brilliant than a thousand suns,
his attempts to translate his experience revealing a
special lunacy from which God rises into the stars
like sparks from burning wood or fleeting passions from a burning
heart.

Credit: NASA/SDO/LRO/GSFC

Waking to Other Voices
by Diane Allerdyce

> *What is metaphor but this fiery explosion under my ribs?*
> *What is the ocean but a place holder for the shore toward which we are pushing madly?*

I
Inside the dome of my waking I hear
light reverberate at the speed of sense
and memory. I wonder at the sheer
coincidence of its strange cadence,
my mother's and father's voices lining
the arch of consciousness, emerging through
whatever I was before, shining
into my waking, burgeoning and new.
Where am I, what am I, alone, adrift
in a universe of light and sound, bright
and yellow inside my mind as I shift
out of dreaming darkness to greet the light?
I rise, walk into the woods outside my door, gift
of nature and meaning, dome of my waking light.

II
When I was a child I woke to other
voices somewhere out there beyond my room,
voices that seemed to have always been there,
voices not only for me but for whom
the arches of the breezeway opened, the door
of my bedroom swinging in welcome, walls
expanding to accommodate the soar
and lift of my discovery, and the calls
of these beings that somehow had entered
my consciousness at waking: the clinking
of coffee mugs in the kitchen, the banter
of aunts and uncles, and I, the thinking,
feeling being I found myself to be,
springing softly toward their security.

III
I wake now to different voices in the house.
As each new sun rises, I send my own
words through waking's veil to the universe,
to say I am here, aware, awake, home
in the envelope of my skin and poised
for anything. I rise to my feet, take
standing, take walking, and find in the moist
forest earth outside this cottage a stake
in creation, where, looking up, I am
so incredibly grateful for the cone
of green branches that form a fringed hem
against the sky of this fortunate dome.
Though I miss the other voices, I feel
their echoes as if still here, and as real.

Credit: NASA Johnson, ISS

Fog
by Gene Martel

Roses are red, but not always; sometimes
they're pink, and sometimes violets are white.
But fog, like ashes long dead, is mostly gray.
A fog is still, but not always. Sometimes
it curls and rolls when chased by puffs of wind.
Fog's life is brief, cut short by sun and breeze,
but not always. On Newfoundland's Grand Banks
a ghostly behemoth billows on the waves,
spawn of Gulf Stream waters and Arctic air.
On lonely seas it broods, but not always.
Sometimes, astride easterlies, it invades,
and into its maw the great island fades.
Then the colossal specter haunts the land,
sometimes for days and weeks—but not always.

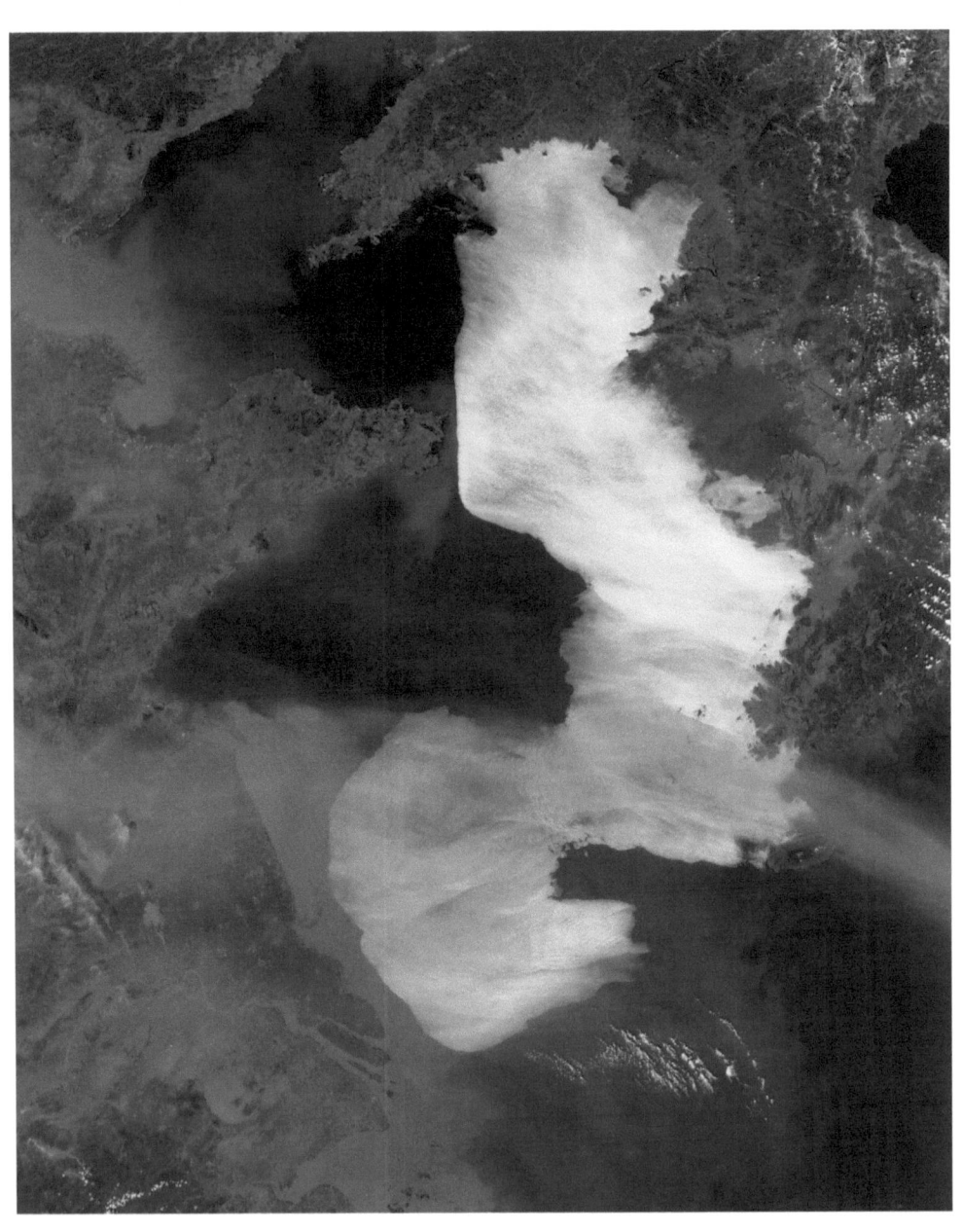

Credit: NASA image by Jeff Schmaltz, LANCE/EOSDIS MODIS Rapid Response.

Gliding Through
by Andrea Best

> *I was reading a book about pleasure,/ how you have to glide through it/ without clinging,/ like an arrow/ passing through a target,/ coming out the other side and going on.*
> —Tony Hoagland, "Impossible Dream"

The morning after
sunlight squeezes through blinds
to touch her damp forehead
like a concerned mother's palm.
In the space between sleep and waking
she is immobilized, terrorized,
locked within an alien body,
unsure if it is dreaming.

When she was a girl
she hid stuffed animals in her bed
pretending they were lovers.
In the prostrate ache of childhood nights,
their reassuring forms
filled the cavernous space
where her sticky secrets
lie awake, whispering.

During her years of clinging to it,
she might have miscalculated.
The arcane equations of pleasure—
a hyperbolic geometry
where bodies curve
away from each other
as the distance grows
from the place
they intersect.

This time could be different.
She could wake and roll
the memory out of her bed,
clearing a space
for new possibilities.
The volume of it
directly proportionate to the mass
of her studied apathy.
Gliding through,
each meteoric pleasure
not an end
but a mere prelude
to the next glittering target
of her affections.

PLANETS

Credit: NASA/JPL

Naked Goddess
by Gene Martel

We call her Venus, naked and goddess skyborne,
uncontested beauty in splendrous light.
We seek, in her, remedy for lovelorn;
we appeal to her for love's treasures at night.
We see apparent magic reach and touch,
enveloping our frailties, making life
delicious, orgasms much too much
to do without, erasing all our strife.
But just as day blots out the night, the real
obliterates the goddess fantasy.
Venus is just a name man used to steal
the wondrous night's universal beauty
to prove fables, but of proof there is lack.

The Venus surface is lava turned black.

Credit: L. Esposito (University of Colorado, Boulder), and NASA/ESA

The Transit of Venus
by Andrea Best

He used to be my density—
like some dark star
swallowing each ray
that might aspire to shine.
He is no sun.
Recognized for influential tides,
the niche cradling his singularity,
bent space accommodates
in time, rendering mine
an eccentric Venus, whose
perfect retrograde revolutions,
once revealing one
slow bright face,
dilate upon encountering
his seductive horizon.
More flesh than holy attraction,
this planet's sharp transit
is Sunday mass
unremembered.

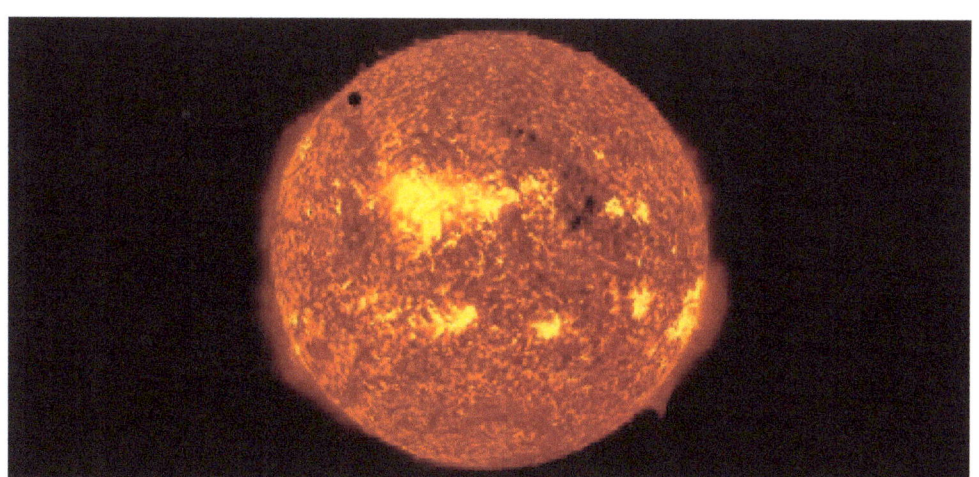

Credit: SDO/NASA

A Dream Magnificat*
by Gene Martel

This place, this planet Mars, it succors us.
This day is God's marvel, the skies azure,
the lands aglory. Our Life here is sweet,
well worth the cramped years in a tube in space.

We had to leave our homes, our native lands.
Our lifestyles, gifts of God, escaped from us,
(the work of Satan's flock, not faithful folk)
we believed, and thus, we knew that we'd be saved

At the end of Earth, that God would find a place
for us in His Great Universe, a new
Eden where all is peace, and abundance grows.
We've colonized His Garden from across

great oceans of space and gathered His promise.
We are His chosen; we owe Him great praise.
Hallelujah! Our planet is not poisoned!
So now, let us sleep and dream in His Peace.

*magnificat: any song, poem, or hymn of praise

Credit: NASA/ESA and The Hubble Heritage Team STScI/AURA

Rogue Planet
by Andrea Best

Gelid giant—
irrevocably adrift,
cast out and alone
in the abyss of
 interstellar space.
Were you once
close to greatness
yet not massive enough
to ignite?
Some inconsequential
brown dwarf—
unknown or forgotten—
persuading no one
to coalesce around
your massive conviction,
amassing nothing
to orbit your
contemptuous collocations.
Obstinate and cocksure,
bending the light
from background stars,
you prove your existence
the only way
you can.

Jupiter shone
by Jeff Morgan

or rather
reflected,
similar to early American writers,
the light of life
and can never break free,
become independent,
but the planet's reaction
this night in the Dry Tortugas,
where if one looks at the stars long enough
the sky and the sea blend together,
is to extend a narrow beam,
creating a walkway across the water
to itself and another world.
No writer,
free to roam the universe of imagination,
could hope to do more,
for Jupiter's art has no intent;
there is no internal source for the art,
only reflection, a setting, and an audience,
me,
who no longer wishes to be a god
to be a god.

Credit: NASA, ESA, STScI, A.Simon, M, via AP

On the Edge
by Gene Martel

We live on the edge among the twigs
near the end of a limb hanging
to the ground, elevating nothing,
uplifting some things, shedding everything,
waiting to dry as do all the twigs.

The limbs, too, will dry and even the tree,
unless catastrophe intervenes
before the drying time. And then, when dry,
we'll break, like twigs and fall to the ground
and become the ground as will the limbs and trees.

And Earth will dry, as will our star, in time.
And after the drying, from the remains
a new star will be and capture planets.
Perhaps, on one of them, trees will grow with limbs
and twigs.

Credit: Norman Kuring, NASA/GSFC/Suomi NPP

A Universe of Corn
by Jeff Morgan

When they awoke, the total lunar eclipse was ending.
The sun's rays shone brilliantly on the edge of the umbra.
Earth, racing around a sun, rotated on its axis.
Their scope leaned forward before the eye,
dangling from the end of a tendon,
and the kernel of the focus was on corn,
miles and miles spread out as the lens drew back;
here and there a modest farm house, barn, and silo
dotted the landscape, surrounded by the corn
that stood in tall uniformed rows.

The house was of weathered wood, peeling and flaking.
The car sat upon cement blocks, rusting and waiting.
Three tired looking humans sat in the dim light of a table
with forks and knives in their hands,
white flags tucked into their throats,
splashing a milky innocence
into their saucer-shaped plates.
A box of chicken nuggets sat at the center of the wooden table.
Another brought over another saucer-shaped plate;
this one full of steaming corn-on-the-cob.

When they zoomed in with their instruments,
they found a dominant isotope.
A carbon atom, C-14,
had colonized the flesh and hair
in *all* of the families
who sat at their dinner tables.
Believing the corn to be the imperialist,
the celestial travelers gathered some maize
and began negotiations for earth's surrender.
The corn would not negotiate,
and as they began preparations for earth's conquest,
their scientists also quickly discovered
the quick and easy energy in corn's high caloric content,
an energy that can be processed
and subsequently consumed in a number of ways,

feeding their bodies and their machines

while the patient corn smiled.

Credit: NASA

SATELLITES

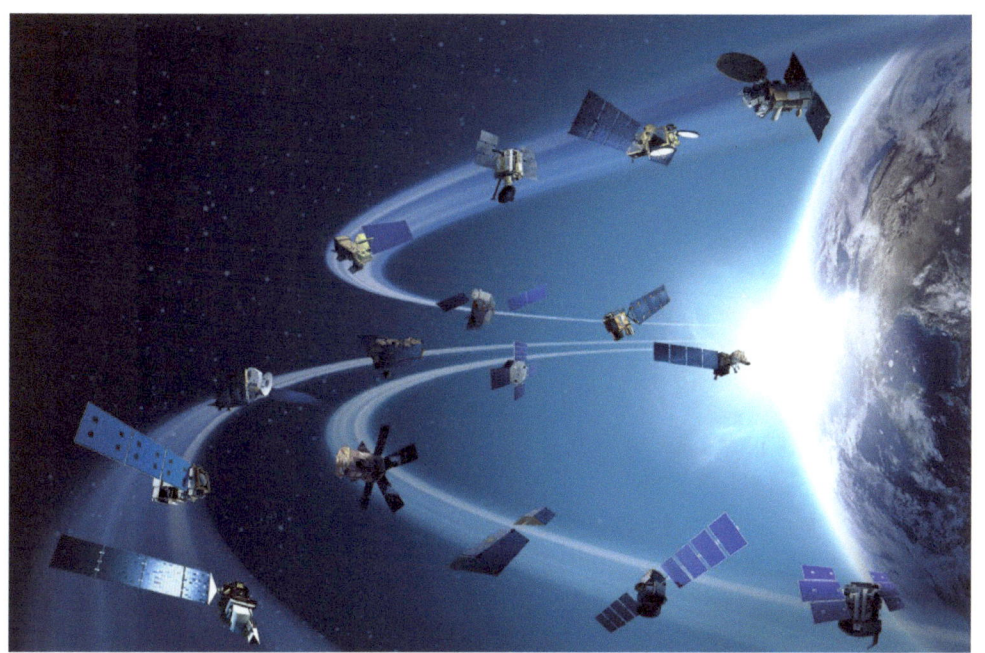

Credit: NASA illustration courtesy of Jenny Mottar.

Quantum Entanglement
by Andrea Best

He did not count on her,
the way she entangles everything:
familiar constellations, unpaid parking meters, brazen limbs—
knitting them gently into her narrative pastiche.
His eager years of experiment and analysis,
countless lists recollected in reverse,
now the subject of her seductive synthesis.
Waxing crescent to waning gibbous,
an aphotic absence spreads between them.
She imagines their particles,
synchronized swimmers in distant waters
perfectly timed sculls and eggbeaters
unseen beneath the surface—
reciprocal toes
pointed in unison
upon detection.

The time before her,
a desperate grasping
in the dark bowels
of opportunistic supercomputers—
their parallel grids networked
to cold calculate probabilities.
Language relegated to
ones and zeroes
inside sterile incubators,
high speed transmissions
replicating some passionless exchange.
Lost were the meanings of things,
the experience of them—
bright taste of strawberry,
heady rush of novelty,
self-conscious delight in a word.

Now, an unforgiving urgency, unspoken
bends the arrow back
to where she boldly revises history—
a new pattern crocheted into

the cosmic fabric, connecting them.
Wrapping space and time
around her instruments,
she hooks him stitch by stitch,
pulling loops through other loops,
a superluminal communication.
The way she strings words like pearls—

his unraveling.

Credit: NASA, ESA, STScI, Jayanne English (University of Manitoba)

Tidal Coupling
by Andrea Best

Ours is a synchronous rotation, my tender gyroscope.
You are always there to steady this impetuous planet.
Though I might prefer to take it to the limit sometimes,
Édouard Roche knows how one disintegrates
when tidal forces exceed self-attraction.
Better that you deliver a steady simmer to my core,
never a boil.

Our celestial dance leaves you transfixed,
gazing admiringly at what has become your whole world.
For what seems like billions of years
a countenance that reveals a mare tranquillitatis
despite the depths of mare crisium
contemplates the cruelty of my naked topography—
out of reach.

The side you cannot show me atrophies
as you forget what you used to know.
You are changed but remain sovereign,
an aging orb that fell
into a rut in this corner of the universe
where you watch me spin
to reveal a proud breast to the sun.
Time will surely slow
this wondering gaze to a steady stare:
two heavenly bodies circling endlessly—

seeing only the other.

Credit: NASA

Panthalassic Embrace
by Andrea Best

The blue vespertine undertow,
guided by some iridescent moon,
pulls pink, fleshy being-for-itself,
nestled and warm within a quilt sewn from memories,
down into this slow dissolution of mind.
Enveloped in watery darkness
eventide, a sensual anesthetic—
freeing in its reassuring regularity
here, diurnal consciousness overcomes will
as listless limbs float to touch the sea
in a Panthalassic embrace
this quiescent suspension,
dormant and lovely until dawn.

The Perpetual Flood
by Diane Allerdyce

> —Well up, pond,—Foam, roll on the bridge and above the woods;
> —black cloths and organs,—lightning and thunder,—rise and roll;
> —Waters and sorrows, rise and revive the Floods.
> —Arthur Rimbaud's Illuminations; translated by John Ashberry

What can we know of what the moon has heard?
Since the caravans left, says Rimbaud, as
The Splendide Hotel was built, there has stirred
myriad grumblings high and low. But has

the silken net the moon has cast revealed
the meaning of the reported grumblings?
Luminescent stones from her rusty shield
extracted—even they are like bumbling

idiots called to testify in courts
banal and ridiculous. At further depths
what we know is less susceptible, less
illuminable by light. Darker forts
than any we have known invite our steps
on ladders leading where we cannot guess.

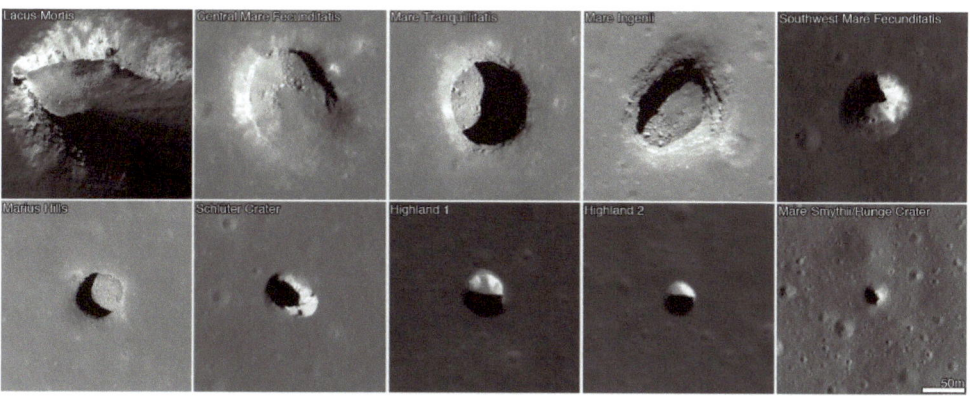

Credit: NASA/GSFC/Arizona State University

Oneness
by Jeff Morgan

It's the first night at home, on the porch, in the swing,
her breasts, developing since puberty for this,
enlarged, milky, the virgin pink darkened,
the nipple, her phallus, sucked, the dilated ducts
issuing into the infant, looking
like neither a boy nor a girl, her breast
pouring out from under her designer sweater,
the one with the design,

                        the snake eating its tail,
and she turns her eyes from the child, eyes closed,
contentment
reigning over the face as after a good shit
or a good fuck, and looks upon the cow,
lounging in the moonlight on the grave of the mother
who died during childbirth so many moons ago,
flicking her tail at a falling ash leaf,
and the child opens an eye to a star
whose wink twinkles in him.

Missing
by Diane Allerdyce

I
You brought white roses on your arm with song,
your smiling eyes the signs of who I know
you are. They're the bright runway lights I long
to follow and merge with each time you go.
You have been travelling too fast too wide,
our spaces expanded too far apart.
When you're here my missing seems to slide
into pushing. When you're gone I feel my heart
opening and closing through the tortured night,
my own resolve to heal conflicted, shorn
of its shimmer, and when I wake the light
I've been chasing through the night is stillborn.
Through the universe forever we've been
missing one another, always, again.

II
At the end of the movie *Shoot the Moon*,
there's a moment when the character
played by Albert Finney, desperate, prostrate,
lifts his arm to reach from the bloodied ground
for his wife, while she, seeing him for whom
she suffered so long so anguished, turns her
face toward her own sorrow, scent of phosphate
filling every crevice with pain, unbound
by protocol, collapsed upon what's left
of everything—a singularity
discovered and discarded as a thought
no longer useful. Here we are too, bereft
of love but still in love, no rarity
in matters that galactic forces wrought.

III
I want to shoot the moon tonight, to feel
my finger on the trigger just as John
Lennon sang in "Happiness. . . ." Moon face
impervious, unmoved by our outcry.
When love shuts its lids against us to seal
off the light, we'll be drifting alone, gone
the final chance to return to the base
of commitment to which we once were tied.
Gone the days of frivolous action,
a wife wearing her child's Wild Western belt
to her husband's prize ceremony, no
spontaneity to gain love's traction.
Now we must live with the cards we've been dealt.
That we dealt them ourselves, my love, we know.

IV
Where are the roses now, my lost, my friend?
I waited for you to return them to me.
I was angry when I left you, but then,
as always, I regretted the harsh fee
my emotions exacted. I can't live
the way you want to live, can't even breathe
in the tunnel you've constructed to give
meaning to your mourning, stage to your grief.
Let me tell you something. I think you know
this already. You are full of sunlight
and stars. The darkness around you can't go
the distance against what is good and bright.
When through the distant universe I send
you a signal, I see the light you lend.

V
In my crystal ball we have succeeded.
We've arrived on the shore toward which we
had been swimming for so long, and it's been
a while since we landed here. We are glad
to be here together, unimpeded
by our past struggles. From our deck the sea
forms a frame to our horizon. And then
there is the garden, the best we have had
of color and beauty, and the promise
of continuing comfort. In summer
and early autumn the evening spreads long
into nighttime, and no Doubting Thomas
peeks over the fence at us, newcomer
to the joy we hear in the shadows' song.

VI
A second wind is blowing, and a third;
seventy times seven, I can feel it
pushing and pulling apart the unstirred
passion of the past to stamp and seal it,
push and steel it, against the lost future
nearly regained. I am tumultuous,
tidal. You are explosive. No suture
can save us from the storm. The tortuous
 outer bands of the hurricane cry out
with rage, protesting all that's in their path,
as if to take it personally, to shout
down obstruction, hiding hurt under wrath.
This is an old wind blowing that commands
us to listen to warnings from new lands.

VII
It is the reckoning of everything,
not the wrecking, that matters. We love
too ferociously, furious to bring
ourselves to recognize the fact, a shove
out of denial and into the truth
that we have always known about our lives,
separately and together, the long tooth
of wisdom and savagery that still strives
to pierce the flesh of indecision, wild
in its unyielding force. It is to know
each other still that we, unbeguiled
and innocent, refuse to let love go,
and in this refusal we stand atop
a cliff above a rushing we can't stop.

VIII
Listen, my love. Listen between the crisscrossed
and perpetually crisscrossing lines of our
own dilemmas and dramas. Like you,
I dreamt that my brother was standing
by me when I was crying and lost.
When I awoke I found him there, a flower
in his outstretched hand for me, and a new
weightlessness on my chest. He was handing
it to me and smiling. That's when I knew
we were going to be okay, you and I,
he, you, and the children too.
Listen, my love. Whatever might ensue
in this crazy, compelling deep night sky,
remember we're only the pre-dawn dew.

Credits: NASA, ESA, G. Duchene (Universite de Grenoble I); Image Processing: Gladys Kober (NASA/Catholic University of America)

EPILOGUE

Credit: NASA, ESA, CSA, STScI

There is Still Love: A Poem for Haiti, January 12, 2011
by Diane Allerdyce

> *If self is a location, so is love:/ Bearings taken, markings, cardinal points,/ Options, obstinacies, dug heels, and distance,/ Here and there and now and then, a stance.*
> —Seamus Heaney

I
When the world falls apart and hearts collide
with the truth and the tragic and shattered
dreams, there rises on the tumultuous tide
of human loss and longing, toward battered
bodies and tender expectations shot
from the sky, a rallying cry, a call
to love and to act with compassion, not
to allow injustice to reign, or fall
into complacence. There are wooden doors
on canvas tents, integrity intact,
while suffering neighborhoods bruise, and stores
of provisions from other lands are stacked.
But hope still pushes through at dawn, above
the smoke-rimmed mountains. And there is still love.

II
When the sky slides under our searching feet
and leaves us lurching in the fall, there are
those who dig in their heels, and those who meet
their cloud-chased destiny head on, on far
horizons of despair. Where is the place
they lost in the trembling? Where are the signs
that all is not forever gone? The face
of the small girl who perseveres and pines
for her lost mother as she's holding tight
to her brother's arm while he leads her from
the rubble, roughshod over piles of blight—
she is a sign and a symbol that, come
what may of sorrow, there's solidity
in love, and substance in the light we see.

III
When the world falls apart and hearts collide
with the truth and the tragic and shattered
dreams, there rises on the tumultuous tide
of human love and longing, toward battered
lives and falling futures, a battle call:
Let us not fail nor let each other fail.
Our responsibility is for all.
Let's put our hearts together and let's rail
to action that is just and true and right,
see in earnest what we are allowing:
real lives lived out in shadows of the humble sight
of tent villages, a disavowing
of injustice, unless we choose to see.
Annou met tèt nou ansanm pou li.

An artist's concept of what a neutron star collision would look like. Credit: Illustration by Robin Dienel courtesy of the Carnegie Institution for Science

The Final Theory
by Andrea Best

Perched on the surface of a brane,
I ponder imaginary time,
contemplate complicit planets
riding gravitational waves while
orbiting some dark mass in a shadow brane.

The weight of eleven dimensions
is enough to crush
a man heading towards
the event horizon—
words caught in his throat
never to escape.

Holding on temporarily,
mind outsmarts gravity,
consigning it to other dimensions.
Perhaps through a worm hole,
the final theory,
his naked singularity,
is only a Planck length away.

To Search the Distant Star
by Gene Martel

My mind expands to search the distant star.
Emergent psyche drifts across the skies,
pursuing worlds where universals are.

The sentient body, static, yearns afar,
as other vision drifts across the skies.
The mind expands to search the distant star.

The social dynamo has left a scar
that putrefies until the soul cries,
and quests for worlds where universals are.

As through a warp in space I wander far.
There some truths I see with startled eyes,
as mind expands to search the distant star.

Perchance I'll learn where right and beauty are.
Perhaps I'll find the court where justice lies,
while seeking worlds where universals are.

I'll return each day to keep the cosmic door ajar,
to catch a glimpse of where the light will rise.
My mind expands to search the distant star,
pursuing worlds where universals are.

Credit: NASA, ESA, J. Dalcanton (University of Washington), R. Foley (University of California—Santa Cruz); Image processing: G. Kober (NASA Goddard/Catholic University of America)

The Missing Link
by Jeff Morgan

Upon opening the book to the map of the brain,
I did not see thought and language.
Perhaps the editor chose that they be uncharted,
leaving the ships to sail without formation;
without a central processor
they should circle in their own circle.

Instead, distant ports are reached,
and the migrations bring forth such a comingling
that the synthetic possibilities seem endless.
The paradox of creation snubs its nose at empiricism,

and we go beyond experience, into space,
where the minutest possible particle
of the cremated remains of a madman
lands on an icy meteor for the miracle.

Is that a single cell I see wiggling there in a most poetic way?

Credit: Bill Ingalls/NASA

Andrea Best is a Certified Deep Transformational Coach and founder of Metamorphose Deep Transformational Coaching who partners with individuals embarking on a transformational journey in support of their self-actualization, creativity, and societal impact. Her career spans both academic and corporate worlds, while her passion for deeper understanding and poetic inspiration expands even further to encompass the infinite and infinitely mysterious Universe.

Her poems have appeared in literary journals *Chiron Review, Florida English, Slipstream*, and *Quest,* and in *Kiss & Tell: Stories of Love, Lies, and Lust Vol. 1,* which was released as an audiobook.

Best completed her Ph.D. at Florida Atlantic University in the Public Intellectuals track of the Comparative Studies program with a concentration in Environment, Technology, and Society, where her research focused on sustainability narratives, the communities of meaning that define them, and their effects on public policy. She also holds a MFA in Creative Writing from University of Miami and a BA in English from Lynn University.

Best resides in the Hudson Valley with her spouse, Madrid-born guitarist-composer-producer Álvaro Domene, who often joins Andrea during live stage performances of her work.

Diane Allerdyce is a poet, professor, parent, partner, grandmother, musician, yogi, and caregiver. Her poems have appeared in *The Ground Up, Feed the Holy,* and *Reflections: Narratives of Professional Helping.*

Diane's creative publications include a chapbook, *Whatever It Is I was Giving Up* (Pudding House, 2007), and an eclectic collection of prose and poetry entitled *House of Aching Beauty* (*EditionsPerleDesAntilles,* 2012). Her stories have appeared in the *North American Review, Stories that Need to be Told* 2022: *A TulipTree Anthology*, and *The TulipTree Review.*

Diane is a faculty member of Antioch University's Graduate School of Leadership & Change. She lives in Boynton Beach, Florida, with her husband Rory, their two cats, and her 90-year-old mother

Gene Martel was born in Springfield, Massachusetts, on May 21, 1930. Embracing a restless spirit, he traveled the world geographically and metaphysically until his death in September 2017, at various times experiencing life as a sailor, student, drill sergeant, consultant, corporate manager, professor, poet, husband, friend, and father of Chloe. Considered to have been a genius by many, he died of Lewy Body Dementia on September 10, 2017, leaving behind over fifty individual poems published in journals and a definitive collection of his poetry entitled *Bones*, published posthumously in 2018.

Jeff Morgan has a book, *Poems Inspired by the Parts of Terry Eagleton's Literary Theory that I Really Don't Understand*, forthcoming from Mellen. Individual poems of his have most recently appeared in *Grist* and *Abandoned Mine*. Morgan is also the author of three books of literary criticism, most recently *The (Un)Welcome Stranger: Intercultural Sensitivity in Six American Novels* (McFarland, 2023), and edited a new edition of Sarah Orne Jewett's *The Country of the Pointed Firs*. He is also the author of many scholarly essays, his work appearing in such journals as *ANQ, Frontiers,* and *War, Literature, and the Arts*. A recently retired educator after 42 years in the classroom, Morgan lives in Boynton Beach, Florida with his wife, Dana.

www.ingramcontent.com/pod-product-compliance
Lightning Source LLC
Chambersburg PA
CBHW042310150426
43198CB00006B/112